SHE WAS MINE

Those who want the rose must
respect the thorn.
- A Fortune Cookie

To the little boy who inspires me daily:

I know life wouldn't be complete without you. You inspire and drive me to be a better woman. Without you and without the unconditional love you give me.... I don't know where'd I'd be. I am grateful and humbled to be in your presence.

I Love You.

Introduction

Who the fuck told my parents it was okay to conceive me? They didn't consider my future bills, student loan debt, the number of heartbreaks I would encounter, or how poor the job market would be for the millennial generation. Remember those conversations as children you had with friends? Talking about what age you'll have children, how you'll be in this excellent fantastic career and your own with no problems? I do, and none of that worked out for me, not even a little. I'm 25; I'm not in my career, I'm considering going back home with my parents; I have a great job I despise, a kid, a shit load of bills and on top of all that include the crappy love life.

I wonder why adults never express how challenging life can be? Is it because they wanted us to view them as perfect or was it to preserve our innocent? Either way, most of them have done a crappy job in preparing us for anything. I can't put all the blame on them because, some didn't have strong examples coming up, and the others were just winging this shit just like us presently.

So, in the mixture of all the adulting and growing up I had to do I also had to grow within myself. Which is pretty freaking hard, I might include. Trying to pinpoint the cause of all the negative energy you're harboring, then figuring out how fucking to correct it and use it to better yourself and yeah this shit really sucks. But, operating in a way that is not favorable to your spiritual growth not only harms you but, those around you as well.

I lay and think of all the screwed-up things I've done as an individual, and I become sad but, only momentarily. I now recognize where I went wrong and what I need to do next time or what to receive from it. Yes, I was shitty, and I didn't care at the time because the world revolved around me and I was the only woman who mattered. Then I faced this unpleasant thing called "growth."

I still understand that growth is not for myself but, it's also for those around me. Being healthy within me will appeal to those who are healthy or encourage those who aren't to get there. By no means is this a GPS to on how to get to a particular sense of "complete" because there is no such concept in this case. As an old acquaintance once stated, "spiritual growth is not a destination it's a journey."

By that she meant the soul, you, are consistently growing and you'll never cease. Whether it's re-learning your needs and desires or developing in a manner to support those around you; you'll always learn a new way to do everything from coping to loving someone to loving yourself, and there will never be a point in your life when you feel so connected that you'll want to stop.

There will be seasons of errors and lessons and boy will the universe give you a million of them. Don't see them as a block in your growth because you are where you're supposed to be at the exact time you're supposed to be there. Nothing in this world blossoms all year round so don't require that for yourself.

It took me 23 years to love myself, and at one moment I couldn't look in the mirror without seeing everything I hated. I've had my experience of depression, pain, suicide, etc. So, by no means will this book make it seem like this journey is a piece of fucking cake. It wasn't, still isn't, and never will be. I've had to pick myself up and put myself together too many times to be thrilled about it.

But, it was all worth it.

25 Is the New 40

So, as stated before I had my life planned out and I was supposed to be in a stable career by 25, married by no later than 35, traveling the world, and a strong maybe on children. Kids were not an option for me back then. Anyway, I had a view of a wraparound porch with a ton of land and a few horses. Yes, I love horses. Seems like a decent life, right? Yep, I thought so too.

Here's what happened in reality, I got knocked up at 19, I didn't complete college, I'm working a job I hate, I've considered being a stripper about seven times a month, I'm drowning in bills, and I am broke also known as living paycheck to paycheck. The only thing I look forward to is happy hour, hot wings, tequila on the weekends, and Saturday/Sunday mornings because I don't have to get up and go to work.

Ask any millennial who is currently "adulting" shoot; you probably agree with me right now. It's funny how none of the plans I made for myself came out the way I wanted. Does that mean I'm upset with myself? No, not at all. But, I can say surprisingly being a mom saved me in more ways than I can ever be thankful. Life huh?

Plans didn't work out for me, and no

matter how many goals I've checked off there's more that I haven't. Goals are something everyone should have but, giving yourself a date or time frame to meet some of those goals is a complete waste of time. Ask those undergraduate students who didn't graduate on the expected date they were supposed to. Which is fine as long as you got your diploma and graduated

I've noticed the biggest problem with having expectations for ourselves are they aren't just for us they are also for those who surround us in life or on the Internet. Don't be that person reading this and say "no not me" hear me out. Most of us do this thing called "comparison" where we take another persons' achievements and compare them next to ours even if it's just for motivational purposes which can be both be healthy and unhealthy for anyone in today's time.

Last year in 2016 I left my job and resigned for a new one which winded up being a fluke. My bills started to fall behind, Christmas was nearing, my son's birthday was approaching, and I went into this spiraling depression. I would scroll social media and see everyone I knew buying a ton of gifts, going out and having fun, looking all glamorous. Then, there was me with this crappy ass bun, no money, a shitty car, no friends, a failing relationship, and my family was driving me insane. To top it all off, it was yet again my birthday. (If you never had a good birthday before then you know what I mean.)

Do you know how it feels to be surrounded by individuals who love you but, always feeling alone? My life turned me towards this dark depression. I couldn't understand why the hell everyone's life was still so perfect. I even tried to commit suicide and failed at it but, the crazy thing is I was sadder that I failed at that too.

I sat in my room for days asking myself how did my life get here and what could I do to fix it? One day I looked in the mirror with tears rolling down my face & wrote on my hand "you're fine" with Kat Von D matte lipstick. After hours of typing notes on my iPhone, I concluded that I needed to stop comparing my situation to everyone else's. No one knew of my downfalls because I never aired them or talked about them.

By, no means was I wishing people were as miserable me. I was comparing my life to theirs wondering why wasn't I in the predicament that everyone on Instagram was. I was blaming myself for everything that had gone wrong over the past months. When I should've been asking questions like "how do I get there?" or "how do I get to see the happiness that everyone is portraying?" Everyone wants everything in their life to seem perfect and put together. They don't want you to know that you had to push back the light bill because money got a little tight. They won't tell you how many times they cried themselves to sleep because they felt their life was falling apart. They won't tell you they had to eat air for lunch because apple music took their last $10. No one wants the world to see their vulnerability. Everyone needs people to look at them and think they are living the life.

Most of us, however, are not. That is okay though I'm not expecting you to live that life if you are kudos to you. For the rest of us, stop pretending that life is perfect for those around you because it's not and nor will it ever be. Life is full of losses and failures which are all okay. Life just is lifeing us sometimes. (Yes I know "lifeing" isn't a word)

We all get so tangled up in this image that none of us sit back and look at the real picture. Life is not going to go the way we want it. It will throw us curve balls and obstacles for everything we need to learn. Life is not a straight path, and if you thought it was supposed to be different, then sorry to break it to you.

There will be a ton of lessons and shortcomings down the road you're on. That doesn't make your chapters any less valuable they make them more interesting. There will be pain, tears, frustrations, and moments when you want to give up, don't. There's this quote from Winston Churchill which states, "If you're going through hell then keep going."

That applies to life, love, and success. Stop comparing your pages to another persons' because being honest you don't know what's in their book and it's not your business to know either. The only pages you can read or write are your own so give yourself a break. You can only do what you can with what you have and if you have little but, are still doing something then congratulate yourself anyway.

Congratulate yourself on everything you do whether it's getting up in the morning, making sure you have a positive day, or something as simple as eating. We sometimes as humans are way harder on ourselves than we need to be because of the people we view around us.

Apparently, we're supposed to have a

perfect credit score, afford $200 dates, own a house and a car, have a degree in whatever field you have gone to school for, a career, and perfect mental health. Oh, you must have all these by at least 30, and at 25 you should have half the list completed.

Now, basing off those around us how unrealistic does a lot of this seem? We're only in our twenties, and most of feel like we're too old not to have it all and too young to have it all figured out. That's only a portion of the pressure we feel today. For those who have children, there is a whole separate expectation, and that's another topic for another day. So, no, everyone is not supposed to have every aspect of their life figured out at such young ages. The only thing you know is rent is due on the 1st, car note somewhere in the mix, and one of these weekends you'll drink just because you had a stressful week.

A comparison is the minds worst enemy. There's this term a friend threw my way called "divine timing," and that how everything happens at the exact time, you are ready for it. You can either pull yourself out of the mud or continue to drown. Trust the universe and its plans for you. I can't guarantee you'll understand the path you're on while on it but, I can ensure it'll click one day.

You're a working progress. Accept yourself.

You Gotta Be Guilty Too

We never look at ourselves as being the culprit for things that happen to us. Think about it, who wants to be the bad guy? The word for this chapter is accountability today sis...

For example, in relationships why is it we never look in the mirror and say "damn, I don't deserve this"? Most of us ask things like "why can't they treat me better" or "why am I not good enough for them." We cant sit and name every wrong a person we've been involved with has done us but, we never talk about how we actually contribute.

Initially, yes we are the victim, and you met

this person, they wooed you and made you feel special, and soon they cheated, lied, or abused you. Now, before I go any further, I fully know abusive and toxic relations are extremely hard to leave. So, do not think I'm insensitive when I say this but, you can't be the martyr to situations you choose to stay in. Whatever reason you have formed is all valid reasons to stay if that's what you wish to do.

We continuously forgive people who have wronged us and somehow, we exclude ourselves from the forgiveness. We allow other people's negative perceptions of who we are trick us into thinking that they are all we will be able to find. Most times we see the best in the people we love and yes we want them to love us better but, you ever had someone mistreat you, and then they get into a new relationship and treat the new person the same way you begged them to treat you? Ha! Hilarious.

At some point, you were thinking "ain't this some shit?" Here's where the accountability comes in because you knew damn well they weren't treating you the way you deserved, and you stayed. Now, they are the "bad guy," and they are but, as are you. People know exactly how to treat others the way they deserve, and sometimes we aren't that one to make them change.

I have been both victim and villain to this. I've treated people like crap and others like royalty. Speaking truthfully, from the victim's standpoint I wasn't doing it intentionally I just became accustomed to being forgiven I didn't feel the need to change.

I believe that the reason we stay is that we understand the people who harm us. We are all capable of being the abuser, and some of us have been that. We understand their darkness because we have a dark side as well. Yin and Yang, you cannot have light without dark and as cliché as that sounds that's why most of us are attracted to chaos.

Ask yourself who were you in your darkest moments and then think about would you have made the efforts to change your circumstances if the shoe was on the other foot? I don't believe any of us a terrible people intentionally, and most of us are only operating in the best way we know how at this point in our life. But, the moment we take a second to reflect on the darker us, the sooner we'll be able to see there's nothing we can do to change someone who doesn't want to be changed.

I don't think we can legitimately understand someone; how they think, feel, and behave and not love them the way they love themselves or see that we've been them and convince ourselves they can change. They can, but only on their terms.

When you think back to the toxic version of yourself, you'll realize that no matter how hard someone loved you it wasn't enough to do better. Understanding that will help you see that you can't save someone who doesn't want to save themselves as well and the longer you play the savior, the less you are the victim.

I can say that savior complex is a bitch but, being a savior means that at some point you have also been the villain and that's partly why it's so hard for us to walk away. Whatever crappy situation you have found yourself in you must understand that with it comes the burden of knowing you've been harming yourself more by staying and you just can't be captain save a hoe.

We blame every outside source for the cause of our pain but, what about us? Because being a villain to yourself is possible. Someone once said to me that the things we love or hate in someone are something we've either did or are doing to another person. Meaning that people are mirrors of us both negatively and positively and the more we run away from our negative mirrors, the more we'll attract the chaos. Simply because, we're blaming them for the pain we endure and want them to be the person who is at fault for our suffering but, in reality, you are both equally contributing to it.

Don't find yourself ashamed of the mayhem because as stated previously a portion of our souls enjoy it. Chaos is poetic. There's a beauty in it that can only be seen in the aftermath. Think of it as an adrenalin rush when you're on a roller coaster. You're excited because that first free fall feels like you're flying. Chaos makes us feel invincible even if it's killing us. Only because if we go through that we can get through anything.

Some battles don't need to be fought it's okay to throw in the white flag. There are four types of people who deal with this; the rejection junkies, the saviors, the complacent, and then the golden trifecta of all three. The rejection junkies look for pain because happiness seems unreal or its the latter that your natural high is coming down because this all seems so surreal. They have become so accustomed to the downfall that feeling poorly seems normal.

The saviors are so used to being drained that it doesn't matter to them how they are affected because they must be the person who brings someone to the light. They don't feel complete unless they are saving a person from themselves. Saviors we can't save everyone.

The complacent are the ones who make excuses for their pain and dwell in it because this is a norm for them. Pain is their void, and without that, they feel lost. They don't care because something is way better than nothing.

To sit and tell you I'm not a portion of all three would be a lie to myself and to what I speak about. I've been the girl who has accepted less. The girl that constantly needed to feel something even if it wasn't healthy. The girl who thought she could fix something that she never broke, to begin with. Then I used all of those situations as some sort of coping mechanism to blame someone else for what I was allowing.

I simply didn't want to face my darkness because I felt it wasn't mine to face. What I didn't realize was that I was the same version of those I blamed... to myself. I laid in bed asking myself over again "how did I get here?" when I realized I could've left a long time ago and been healing already. It hurt me to realize that I was somewhat accountable for the pain I felt so, instead of looking inward I looked outside to blame rather than being accountable too. Being a savior, rejection junkie, and a complacent allowed me to form the idea that I had to stay. I didn't.

Everything started and ended with me.
I now see that I was the only savior I needed.

People Are Not Coping Mechanism

Why are most of us, such serial monogamist? You don't have to be in a "relationship" to be a serial monogamist either. Most people I know, including myself, have jumped into the arms of another person before we've even breathed from our last relationship. I've done that more times than I'm proud to admit. Whether we're using people as a coping mechanism, out of boredom, or because some of us can't fucking be alone, we've all done it at some point.

Prime example. One summer I met this girl, and we hit it off. We exchanged numbers, conversations were fascinating, our birthdays weren't far apart, and we had more things in common than most people I knew.

Eventually, the relationship between us grew into something more than platonic. The sexual chemistry was somewhat real and I at the time was going through a rough time relationship wise. We all know where I took things next. I knew deep down inside I wanted nothing more than what we were doing because I was still in love with someone else but, denial kicked in. She was great. Perfect even. But, it was wrong time and the wrong place. I was ignoring what I knew would be right for not just myself but, her too and continued to do what felt right.

Here's why I was wrong though, I didn't consider the person who was building a bond with me. I kept telling myself I had things under control and everything will be okay. Little did I know I was completely wrong.

She invited me to come to her hometown for a weekend of fun. Even though every bone in my body told me not to go, I went anyway. It was a great weekend. We explored, she took me to her spot, ate great pizza, and had sex. Great fucking sex. I left Sunday afternoon drove home and ended up having to pick between my heart and something that could have been good for me but, I knew it wasn't what I wanted.

Well by this conversation we all know what I picked. I can't say everything I did was intentional because it wasn't. But, everything I did was because I wanted to and did not care who was in the crossfire. Actually, I don't think I considered the crossfire because I was selfish and I caused a lot of damage.

How can one person cause so much damage at one time? Well, because I dragged my bullshit into the sheets of another person who was fine before I walked in. She was a comfort for me, a breath of fresh air, a friendly conversation, and an incredible orgasm. My heart just was not there for grabs. Shit, I didn't even have it myself to give away.

We need to stop using people as coping mechanisms because we're lonely and we don't know how to sleep alone. Stop ruining good people because we are hurt. Hurt people only do one thing in this world, and that is hurt other people. I would know because that is what I did to more than one person at a time. People say "the best way to get over someone is by getting under a new person." Well, I'm here to say no you are toxic and you are wrong.

People don't allow themselves to heal and when you don't give yourself time to heal you bring over issues from former relationships like insecurities, trusting, or having up walls that you're probably making impossible to break down. Having a guard up is okay because no one will care for you better than yourself but, to have up guards and give people the run around is not.

We have all at some point, or another have destroyed people we have placed everything and vice versa. At some point, we have to stop playing the victim and fix ourselves to receive the love we deserve. The universe will not give us what we've been praying for until we feed your soul. Sit down and analyze why the hell we allow so many toxic people in our lives and why we spread toxicity to people who are good to us? We all have fucked over the nice guy because they were "too nice." Believe it or not, it is a thing.

If you know that you're not ready for

genuine love, give that shit to yourself and don't waste anyone's time. If you know you have 50 walls, two locked doors, and a chamber with a fingerprint lock guarding your heart do not go and fall into the next person's life. If you know you're madly in love with another human being, don't lead anyone on. We know deep down in our hearts we are not ready but, we're so terrified of being alone that we'll go with whatever comes your way to feel something. It is a human instinct to yearn for affection and love. Those are desires we all want to, and they're also desires that can fuck you up too.

I see a cycle that even I once was in, of us hopping from person to person because they make us feel good. Stop doing that. We will never find what we're looking for until we have given it to ourselves and we can't place our home in the arms of another person because the foundation should be within us and us only. You are your own home, and it is okay to feel safe and warm with the comfort of yourself.

Now, for those of who are caught in the crossfire you are not innocent. There will be a million red flags that go off when dealing with a broken person. Do not think you can fix everything because everything is not for you to fix. It is not your job to always be the shoulder to cry on, the person to remind them of their worth, the person to help them fix the pieces that have were broken since you said hello.

You may be ready to love this person and may see the potential in them they don't see themselves. But, that's what they are, potential. The canvas isn't complete, and you don't always need to be Picasso. Sometimes, you have to see the painting for what it is, fragments. An incomplete fucking picture. You know the outcome will be beautiful but, the finished product isn't always your trophy to win. Accept that.

Sometimes, we put ourselves in the crossfire without questions because we can see the capability of someone. Just remember it is okay to ask a million questions because you have to protect yourself. Most times, people operating out of hurt don't realize that they are and that's where you have to step in and be the boundary before more than one person is affected. Most importantly yourself.

Realizing the person you want sometimes doesn't deserve you and not because you're too good for them but, because they aren't ready for you and what you have to offer. Remember some people can deal with all of this and heal broken people, and that's great. If you are that person be wary of the ones, who are making the efforts to change and the ones who are complacent in their pain.

The people who no matter what you do to guide them they will not allow you to be there. You'll have to deal with a million issues you did not cause because that person hasn't given themselves room to breathe or asses that maybe they are a tad bit fucked up. We look for the love we didn't get in recent situations from people who can't give it to us because they don't have it themselves to give.

It's all a cycle, and the once happy individual is now the one battling a broken heart, unanswered questions and the feeling of being lonely.

Remember not everyone that is damaged will be this way so, don't think that. That's not the case at all there will be people who are healing themselves and also can manage another person in the mix. What you as a healer, because we are all healers to someone, needs to do is learn when to be patient with a person and when to cut them off for your sake and sanity.

Expiration Ain't Just For Food

One day I was scrolling through twitter, Dyke twitter that is. I ran across and tweet from a fellow tweeter, Kween. She said, "people need to learn when to stop staying past their expiration dates." For some reason, that resonated deeply. I had been going through a tough time, and it felt like I needed to see that exactly when I did. (divine timing)

I realized I was holding to certain things/people and was terrified to let them go. Platonic or romantic, I have this weird habit of "people hoarding." I was willing to accept things from past situations I was uncomfortable with because I could not take their services to my life was done. I was no longer in the safe spaces.

I would do things like sending long drawn out texts trying to figure out where relations I was involved with had gone wrong. I needed anwers to why nobody ever stayed. I've lost friends, and I've lost lovers. Shit, I lost myself trying hold on to them.

I guess I was looking for some closure in our relationships. The thing is closure is not real. You'll always want more reasons why you aren't "good enough" or why a person no longer needs you.

The only thing you need to know is, you and that person have reached your expiration dates. You two no longer serve a purpose for one another. Your chapter has been completed.

The sooner you accept these things, the more accessible you're healing process will be. We tolerate anything from people we love because something is better than nothing. It's not, and you never really have nothing when you have yourself. We as people look at love as this unconditional bond and sometimes it is but, are you hurting at the same time? For me and others who love deeply, once we love you, we'll always love you but, can we learn to love ourselves as much? When is it time to accept that some people we love can be loved at a distance?

Yes, heartbreak is pain that you feel mentally, physically, and emotionally. Some of us lose weight from not eating, hair starts falling out, we're crying every other 5 minutes, and to top it off you see the people you love living life like its golden. You spent youre time pouring your affection and love into them while they're pouring into themselves or other people. You have convinced yourself it's okay because you love this person and you need to know you've "given your all." Not only have you given more than you should've they aren't even asking you to continue to give.

Love is not enough to put yourself on the back burner for another person.

Especially, if that person is no longer reciprocating those same efforts that you are. You're only prolonging the inevitable for you and hindering your healing process. Heartbreak is just someone beating you to the punch first. Once you've gained all you need to learn from a person let the universe guide them out no matter how it hurts.

We are here to learn from the permanent people, and those who also expire from us. Did you cry over spoiled milk? If you did what did you learn from it?

I had to learn from heartbreak that I could not treat people any way I wanted to. I'm not stating that how I have acted in the past was right. It was wrong but, if I knew better, I would have done better.

When you hit that "what in the entire fuck" stage in life, and you're sitting on top of unfolded jeans using them to blow your nose you begin to reflect on all the shit you've done to all the people who love and care about you. You think what your doing is okay and I'm a great person and vice versa for anyone I've encountered. It's just different people bring out different sides to you. Doesn't excuse the behavior, we just do things and say things to make ourselves believe that the way we're operating is the right way. I don't think that we are all ourselves. We are the people we love, the people we hurt, and the people who love us. Shoot, sometimes we even pick up pieces of strangers in random convenient store conversations.

You hear nothing or meet no one on accident.

I read this book, and it explained how our souls connect with people who have what we need to help our spirit grow in ways we can't do for ourselves. You will be a stepping stone for some people and other times you will need one.

Sometimes, people see who you are for each other before you do.

But, once the lesson is learned you have to let that person go. It'll take you a while to accept things for what they are but, once you see the bigger picture, the rest will fall in line. Every situation starts off with the magical experience that consumes you. Your entire world feels perfect, and you've fallen so deep that you ask yourself is this even real?

Yes, those emotions you feel are 100% authentic, and mostly it's reciprocated. Even more magical, right? Then, there's a spark in you. You feel yourself changing, and those around you notice how much you're growing. So, time goes on, and you're becoming a new person and while you're growing your partner is growing and simultaneously and you're both trying to learn yourself and each other.

Often, you grow into two different people. Your wants, desires, and needs change. Which are beautiful but that doesn't mean it'll help you develop together?

I get it, the absence of a person you love is hard accept but, the more you ignore the signs that you're both growing differently the harder the separation will be. Once you view things outside the emotional aspect you'll realize that what you had was not all that great shoot, maybe it was even a little toxic.

Don't kill yourself trying to be a part of someone's life because you don't know how to walk the hell away.

There are 7 billion people on this planet, and someone will be willing to eat your ass like groceries and, one of these individuals will accept you and everything that comes with you.

The errors, the pain, the flaws, all. Be patient

What Do You Expect?

So, we all have heard the term "expectation" right? We all have some form of expectations in our life whether it's for ourselves or the people/things we surround ourselves with. But, as William Shakespeare once said: "Expectation is the root of all heartache."

One of the hardest lessons I had to learn is that expectations only form an idea for us and not the people we have in our lives. Most of us, have some unrealistic view of how things or people should be but, who are we to determine how someone presents themselves to us is wrong? Often, we get upset at other parties because they haven't conformed to whatever ideals that we (emphasis on we) have believed to be right.

Now, do not confuse having standards with having expectations because they are two entirely different concepts. Let me explain, standards are things like being a good person or having manners when going out on dates. Expectations are roles that we expect people to fill like being hopeless romantics to fit your idea of romance.

I am a hopeless romantic, and I can

admit I have very unrealistic ideas of romance but, I'm also a realist, so I know that when people don't live up to the role I placed on them, it's not their fault because that's not who they are. I remember once, getting a text message from someone I was dealing with at the time asking me why I don't send thoughtful, good morning text when I wake up. I was baffled by the question because I am a romancer but, I don't open that portion of who I am for just anyone that crosses my path. I responded with "well, why would you want me to send you something I don't mean?"

I had been placed in a role that I never asked to be in. I had never sent a heartfelt good morning text so why was I being required or requested to do so when I had been giving the same Tatyanna since the beginning. Then it dawned on me that it wasn't me who couldn't live up to the role but, it was them who expected me to be someone I wasn't because they thought it would be special for them.

Listen, everyone gives or shows you exactly who they are the moment you meet them. Whatever you decide to place them in is on you but, don't be upset when they can't live up to it. Granted, we all have been here, myself included, but, think about it, do you think that situations could have been better had you accepted the person for who they were instead what you made them be?

Given the right time and person, whoever it is, will evolve at their own pace. What you think they should be or become isn't up to you and sometimes it just isn't you that they change for. There are so many unwritten rules to dating and friendship that it's hard to depict what is right and what is wrong. There is no right or wrong in this even if we do make up "rules" as we go.

If you want to set expectations, I suggest setting that you expect yourself to accept people for who they are and not who you want. People will be people, and that's just what it is. What you choose to accept from them is your decision but, you can't make someone fit your role because you see them in a different light.

I was always placed on a platform that I didn't want to be in at one point. I was seen as this guru who people run to for advice or the fixer-upper to others problems, and I felt I wasn't. I'm me, and I'm learning just as much as the next. This book isn't a guideline; it's me sitting at a computer screen typing to myself and talking myself through my healing hoping that anyone else who is in my shoes can learn from me as I am doing.

I don't know everything, and I am

perfectly okay with that but, most people believe that I do. The platform that I was placed in is something I've grown to own because it's a role I've accepted and a position I'm kind of good at. Do I have my moments? Yes, just like the next but, if I didn't want to give anything I don't want to I don't fucking have to. It all boils down to people do doing what the fuck they want to do regardless of what you say or believe.

It took me some time to realize that I was hurting myself by expecting people to be the person I am to them to me. I'm a romantic ass woman, and you know some people aren't. Does that mean that I will find another passionate ass woman to match my energy? Hopefully yes but, if not that's perfectly okay. People are out here peopling, and yes, that's a term I just made up, so who am I to force someone to conform to me?

It is human nature to yearn for specific forms of intimacy (Are you human if you don't?) But, we must learn that our desires do not overpower who someone is or who they give us. We want them to evolve but, not at the expense of someone else's request.

Taking what we are given and expecting nothing less or more from the people who are providing to us is the end goal. I can't determine who I'm going to grow into because I'm continually evolving myself so, I can't decide that for others.

Whether it is dating to marry, being an unrealistic hopeless romantic, or just expecting too much 9/10 they're all disappointments that you lead yourself into. The quicker you realize that nothing you expect is a guarantee, the sooner you'll be able to let things flow the way they are supposed to.

Do not confine yourself either because expectations for yourself are just as harmful to those you set for others. It's okay to have standards and to desire things. Just keep the realization that not everyone can meet the bar you set, including yourself, and give everything time to play out the way that it should turn out is better than trying to control the outcome.

Everything you want doesn't always end up being everything you need, and people are the prime example.

Expectations apply pressure, and sometimes, people we don't think can fold, actually do.

The Art of Detachment

My mom told me a story about me having a pacifier when I was a baby and when I lost it, I cried for two weeks. According to her, I didn't want any other pacifier but, the one I was given. She stated she had gotten me several pacifiers and for some reason, I knew that none of those was the one I had formed an attachment to…. We all know where I'm going with this.

Why is it that we form attachments to

things and people? Why is it that we cannot just enjoy things as they are or as they are given to us? For example, why do we get addicted to the idea that someone we encounter will be in our lives forever? It's like we modify our entire future based on some fabricated notion that the people we meet are permanent. We can never enjoy people for the moments they are meant to be in our life. We presume that whatever reason they entered it was some divine intervention and we subconsciously need them to stay around to validate us.

People will come and go faster than we can blink our eyes. They can be there for a plethora of reasons, and instead of enjoying their presence we imagine a life planned out with them involved.

Learn to let people in and let them leave when they are supposed to. I'm also saying that to myself.

I remember planning out my entire life with people I've allowed to come into my world. The result never ends the way I imagine, and then I was stuck with feelings that only I have and a shit ton of disappointments that I created for myself. Attachment is a form a co-dependency, and we depend on these people to be our emotional outlets, diaries, some even use others for financial support. Whatever reason you've formed an attachment to these people know that they do not fucking belong to you and when they are ready to leave there is nothing you can do to stop them.

Most people are lessons, and that's the harsh reality. We give people too much ownership of our lives that we lose ourselves in the process. Stop attaching your heart to things that are meant to come and go because the truth is people come and go.

I know, it's hard because some people ignite a fire in us that we have a hard time igniting ourselves. I have had someone light my world on fire but when you place everything you have into someone else what will you be left with once they go?

The answer is nothing.

Who are we to hold people hostage because of co-dependency? First of all, the shit is unhealthy to expect someone to stay because we have formed an ideology that we can't live without them. We can, and it's toxic to place the burden (yes I said burden) of forcing (yes I said forcing) someone to stay because we've attached ourselves to them without even getting permission to do so.

Who we are is not defined by the people we encounter we are bits are bits and pieces of them but, they do not belong to us. It's okay to let them leave traces of themselves on us and still not feel lost when they leave and that my friend is the art of detachment.

Embrace the time you have with the people you surround yourself with because at some point they will leave us because death is inevitable. Live in the moment and not in the future of what we want from people because them leaving or staying is not up to us.

You'll remember every intimate detail between you two. But, it's all memories, an example of pure happiness, and a guideline to what you should feel with people you love. Attachments don't just come in physical forms either. We all have some attachment to how we should be or how our life should be when in reality most of us are just winging the fuck out of it.

It's beautiful to live in the moment and the space that we've created for ourselves and others. It's freedom to live and let live without hoarding ideologies that people belong to us.

Don't break your own heart because you're keeping something that doesn't need or want to be kept.

Reciprocation? Wanted but, not mandatory

We as people have formed this idea that the way we feel towards certain people means they have to feel the same way but, reciprocation is not compulsory. How many of you have dealt with people you know like you way more than you'd like to allow yourself to believe? I have, plenty of times. How many of you used the "I'm just not ready for the emotional commitment" phrase and continued to entertain people who you know feel the exact opposite? I have. Here's the thing though you're not entitled to reciprocate that emotion but, you should cut people off when you know the relationship is taking a left turn. Sometimes, we have to do the work for the other person.

People think that as long as you make things clear about how emotionally unavailable you are it is enough. Unfortunately, that is not the case. Enough is not being available at all because most of the time our actions do not match our words. We do things like go on dates, talk on the phone all night, and other romantic stuff that emotionally unavailable people aren't supposed to do. Before you know it you're being asked for a commitment that you know you have no desire to be in. Whether you're just not interested or you're healing from a past love. Be honest with yourself and all parties included. That does not mean reminding the other party how you're "not ready" and how you "don't want any attachments" because if that were true, you'd focus on yourself.

On the flip side, people say they want complete honesty but, only when it benefits their wants and desires. Can you handle the truth? The honest, raw truth? The reality that the person you want isn't ready and more than likely won't be for a long time? No, most times you aren't because oddly, people love emotionally unavailable people. No one I've encountered liked rejection from someone they felt feelings for first. You get upset because you have been "led on" when in reality the only person who led you on was yourself. Both parties are completely wrong in the situation though. The not ready individual reminded you of how much they aren't ready but, stayed the night 4 nights out of the week, went on dates with you, introduced you to their life and once you opened up, they hit you with the "Oh I told you I wasn't ready months ago" line. Complete bullshit.

The "you lead me on" party is wrong because you expected reciprocation when there was none. You thought you could change their mind. Maybe even the thrill of the challenge aroused you to stick around. Here's the thing, you stayed. Your decisions were your own, and you can't play the victim but, for so long even if their actions didn't match their words, they told what it was on their end from the beginning.

We are emotional people, and we all crave some sort of intimacy at some point or another. A lot of us do and say things out of a response because a person makes us smile or they're "good" for us so, we react to emotions portrayed. Still fucked up but, it's the truth.

Situations like this suck because somebody "has" to be the bad guy. Its human nature to blame and most times it's the person who stated they were not ready from the beginning which is fine because being the bad guy is better than prolonging someone you have no intention to hold on to.

To those who feel lead on remember, not every flower or leaf in nature is meant to be touched. Poisonous flowers do exist.

It's beautiful at times, exquisite even, but, it causes more pain touching rather than observing. Some things won't be meant for you, and that is okay. Especially the people who aren't ready for what you have. You can bring everything to the table but if someone doesn't want to eat with you, they won't.

Respect people who honest enough to tell you these things even if their actions don't match their words. Yes, I agree that's shitty, and It's easier said than done but, at least they were continuously honest.

Look, we all want reciprocation from people we've allowed in our realm. Once again, reciprocation is not mandatory, and you'll kill yourself trying to figure out why you aren't good enough.

You're good enough for you. You're good enough to reciprocate the same love you're projecting to yourself. The why's, how's, and what if's are not there for you to decode. Human instinct will kick in, and you will ask those questions, it's a given. The sooner you accept not everything needs an answer, the sooner you'll be okay.

Stop expecting people to love or like you the way you do and then allowing yourself to feel "used" or "led on" because they don't. Also, stop giving people sweet nothings if you have no intention of catching them when they fall.

Sometimes, you're not that person's cup of tea. But, you are someone's Henny straight so, don't forget that.

The thing about reciprocation is it's terrific. It's a beautiful feeling to have the atmosphere feels the same way when you're in each other's presence. To know that the person you're willing to catch will not drop you either. Trust me; I get it. I've felt it before but, you won't feel that with everyone you encounter.

Certain aspects of your love need to

remain just that…. Yours. Not everyone will reciprocate what you feel or what you want from the relationship you both share. That is fine everything is not meant for you to have. I have this prayer I say:

"God, please don't allow my heart to get attached to things that are not written in the stars for me."

Think of things with a silver lining complex. Yeah it's crappy that you have all the feelings that aren't returned but, you're King/Queen is waiting for you out there and like all of our elders say "patience is a virtue."

It sounds so cliché but, the slogan is always right.

Old Wounds Don't Need Your New Apology

During this journey, I wanted to apologize for all my wrongdoings. Honestly, my desire to apologize was entirely too late for other people to care and it wasn't like I wanted to rekindle any old flames or friendships. Well, friendships yes, the old flames not so much. I sat and typed rough draft after rough draft trying to find the words to say to everyone. Then, it hit me, and I realized my apologies were fucking selfish. It wasn't to make things right or to make amends I wanted to clear my conscious and feel better. Being truthful I probably wouldn't have thought about apologizing until what was done to me caused me to see what I had done to others.

Most people don't even want an apology after three years has passed, and most people also don't want to be reminded of how you hurt them. If they're anything like me they probably already forgave you and moved forward with their life. The apology you want to give isn't genuine, and you're looking for some form of a verbal confirmation that all is forgiven.

Isn't that guilt a bitch though? You sit and think about how you're feeling, and you can't fathom the thought you made some else at some point in your life feel the same way. But, the silver lining is it's also a sign of growth which is beautiful but, keep other people out of it.

Just imagine, one day you're happy, and everything in your life is going well. You're eating again, you're sleeping again, and then you get an email at 2 am with a long drawn out apology from someone who harmed you three years ago. Most people would wonder why the hell now and what is causing you to apologize after so long. Then, they'll scroll your social media and see a bunch of heartbreak and confusion and realize you got a dose of your own medicine.

Unfortunately, most people don't learn a lesson until it smacks them in the face. Until they're holding themselves at night apologizing for causing the pain, they feel on anyone else. Face full of tears and a mind full of "what the fuck do I do now."

The con about old apologies is that you never know if that person or people have healed from it. Humans can fuck people up so, being as though you don't know what state they're in do you believe it is a good idea to possibly re-open old wounds?

As a kid when you scrapped your knee playing outside you would go in the house, your mom would pour peroxide on it, stick a band-aid on it, and you would continue to play outside. If the scrape was big enough, it was hard to bend your knee for a few days, and this ugly scab would grow over it. It would itch and sometimes even bleed because you were doing too much.

Now, imagine someone coming to rip the scab off, and you have to start from square one. A new band aide, more peroxide, and more pain because scar tissue hurts a bit more when it has to re-heal. Old apologies open old wounds that most people have already moved on from, healed from, or suppressed because they got sick of crying every day.

Recently, I had an old flame reach out to me apologizing which, was weird because that was the same person I, myself, wanted to apologize to. I realized how wrong I had done them, and for some reason, they blamed themselves for what transpired between us. So, at that point, I had to sit and have a talk and tell them that it wasn't them. I was just a shitty person, and what they did while we were in dealings I honestly didn't give a fuck.

But, that was my moment to apologize as well. I already undyingly needed to right my wrongs so why not take it? At that moment, the window was open, and I was given a chance to apologize because the apology was wanted. I'm saying this by saying I don't mean never to apologize. Just don't be sorry when no one asked you. Not everyone you feel guilty about hurting wants to be reminded of the damage you've done. Especially if they've moved on and everything is now a memory. Don't pull the Band-Aid off to find out how the scar healed.

Apologies only bring back "what if's" and "why's" answers neither party need unless rekindling old flames. Which if you're genuinely just apologizing out of guilt then reviving anything is not in your agenda right now. Whatever karma you think you've caused for yourself you got it already.

You don't need a discussion with anyone to forgive yourself. The other person more than likely forgave you long ago whether consciously or subconsciously. You had to hit rock bottom to start brand new, and it sucks but, don't bring someone into something that's made for you. You were not perfect, and you should not allow yourself to suffer forever due to mistakes you made in the past.

You realize the error of your ways, and now you want to pop up and apologize to release whatever karmic energy you think you've caused. That apology is not changing a damn thing. The best thing for you to do is apologize to yourself for them. It took months to clear my conscious on my own. I made a few bumps, dragged people along the way, and moved on with no worries, and that's called human instinct.

Accountability, apologies, and accepting. Three "A's" I call them. You're taking ownership of your actions however long you took to do so. Now, you want to fix everything, you realize you can't, and you accept everything for what it is. That forgiveness you're trying to find you already received. You don't need to hear the word "forgiveness" to be forgiven.

Even if the other party hasn't forgiven you no amount of forgiveness will matter until you accept things for what it is. You fucked up in the past, learned your lesson, and now it is okay.

Keep your remorse to yourself.

Pedestal Aren't For Love

We have a habit as humans of placing how we love others on a pedestal we don't always deserve. You know how we are; most of us believe we're phenomenal lovers and we don't contribute to any downward spiral in a relationship.

Some of us aren't the lovers we think we are. Myself included.

I hear people say "the love I give is unforgettable" or "you can leave but, you'll never find what I gave you elsewhere." Most times, we give little to nothing to people we are in relations with due to complacency or knowing our partner. You ever had someone who wooed you in the beginning, and a year into the relationship they stop making an effort or things get "boring" for lack of better words? What's the saying? "Continue to do everything you did to get her to keep her."

That's not saying you aren't capable of being the phenomenal lover you know you can be because, you've been that person. It's just human nature to get comfortable and you don't think about date night often because you've gotten accustomed to just existing in each other's space. The excitement is gone and sometimes with that along follows the extra effort.

I saw a post from a former lover, and it said they had found someone who genuinely loves them. You know what? After seeing multiple posts, I couldn't do anything but agree. I couldn't believe I of all people did not love someone how I thought I was. Again, I became complacent, and romance faded right along with the excitement of new love. You know, the honeymoon stages. I found myself grateful the person saw the happiness I didn't give them.

It sucks though because before that you couldn't tell me I wasn't the worlds most engaged and best lover. You couldn't tell me I didn't go above and beyond for anyone blessed with the presence of my love. I wasn't a crappy lover so please don't read out of context. I just wasn't as great of a lover I could've been or was before.

I became lazy, and that's the hard truth.

There's this term that flies through dyke twitter called "love languages." Which means in a roundabout way how you receive and give love, and it can vary from words of affirmation, physical touch, etc. What I also learned was we as people don't acknowledge how someone we're involved with receives love. We give them what we feel is right for them and that's not how it's supposed to work.

I don't regret or a wish I could've seen what I know now sooner. No, not at all. It's the realization that maybe Tatyanna is not the perfect lover and I contribute to downfalls just as much as the next person.

Learn your love languages and learn the love languages of those who you're involved with both platonically and romantically. I learned that love abstract and how you give love or lack thereof doesn't make love negative all around it's just a negative experience. It's not our job to provide ourselves with the trophies of loving someone; it's the surrounding people that gives us the pedestal. They determine if our love was grand to them. They decide whether we're giving love correctly.

Who are we to tell someone else the way we loved them is the right way? We all have this thing called ego, and some of us are also stubborn so, we ignore our loved ones when they tell us what they want from us or how they want to be loved. Because we have formed this egotistical idea that our love cannot be found anywhere else which is true because I believe no two people view/receive love in the same way. But, that doesn't mean there isn't someone who is better suited to love them.

Here's a perspective change. You ever heard of "the one that got away"? There are people from my past who have resurfaced and stated things like "I haven't found your love elsewhere" and it's disturbing in some sort. It rubs me the wrong way because I don't want to be the comparison to your next or current lover. I don't want to be the platform of the love you feel you cannot find anywhere. There's no picture perfect idea of what love should or could be. The only comparison I want you to have is finding someone who loves you better in ways that your last couldn't. Because that's the goal and the only comparison that should be invited into your life.

You'll push away people who could love you in ways your former couldn't because you placed that love on a pedestal. You allow that person to be viewed so highly you never give another love its chance. It's not fair to those you're engaging with but, it's also not fair to you to dwell on someone else's love because you think what they gave you is irreplaceable. It is.

The only situation I could ever see that making even the slightest of sense is if your lover passed away. Even then the love isn't irreplaceable it's just different. People get so hung up on soul mates that they don't see you have a plethora and not just romantic either. Maybe that love was good for you because you needed an example of love to be shown so, you can give it. Perhaps that love was just a conduit to open sides of you thought weren't accessible.

Dwelling on the would've, should've, & could've only hindered your allowance to receive blessings and your ability to move forward. I don't want to be guilted with the fact that someone feels they cannot move forward or find what they want in someone because they stuck me on some magical pedestal of the ideas that my love is irreplaceable. I don't want to be irreplaceable to someone I no longer have in my life.

Just because it doesn't work, that doesn't mean you will never be happy again. People are either lessons, blessings, or a mirror. Everyone has room to grow, especially within the love topic. Everything is based on love languages and learning how to love your loved ones the way they see fit.

We can be selfish in our views, and we can think a little too highly of ourselves because we don't think we love wrong.

But, sometimes we do, and we sit back and realize maybe we aren't the perfect lover and it's okay.

Sometimes people, including ourselves, don't have the range to love each other in ways we need. That is also okay.

Too Much? Pssh

I cut myself purging again
Gutting my fickle fortitude.
Terrifies you'd get caught in the thick
of me
I rearrange
I seen, saw, and swung it
Reduced me to rumble
Found me easy to navigate
said feet feel better on beaten shoulders
head stays steady on other body
shoulders.
How me too me for you?
When you decide, I need tailoring

I soon let you sow into me
never willing to recognize the reap.
An unrecognizable shadow shifts
beneath my feet.
Hungry hollow hangs
Tryna get full of myself.

- Eb

All my life I've been told I am "too much." I've been too emotional, too sensitive, too nonchalant, too talkative, etc. As I've gotten older, I realized I've been apologizing for who I am because I've been too much for the wrong people. We train ourselves to think who we are is a burden to those around us. That we are entirely too much to handle and we are not. You were just too much to someone who couldn't handle you.

Granted I can be a bit dramatic but, this is something I know very well about myself.

I know when I am dramatic, and I know when someone is disregarding what I feel because they don't want to understand. There comes a time in life where we have to stop apologizing for caring, being sensitive, or emotionally inclined. Stop apologizing for every sentence you say, trust me I know, I've been there. You make a corny joke, and you apologize for being "too nerdy." You laugh at something in one of those "ugly laughs," and you apologize for laughing that way.

Apologies are only meant for things you should be sorry about, and you should never be sorry for you. I've spent so much of time tiptoeing around people because I can come off too strong or dimmed my light down because sometimes I'm just too damn bright. I've apologized for thinking I'm attractive or good at what I do. I've given so many people the power to tell me who I am or what I should act like in public. Those people don't like the true you. They don't like the Harry Potter references or the fact you sometimes snort when you find something hilarious. They don't want you to own your space and be comfortable in who you are.

You ever held a conversation with people and found out your views were a tad bit different and you didn't speak up because you know you'd apologize for having a different viewpoint? You ever found yourself not engaging in specific conversations because you seem "too passionate" about the subject? I have on more occasions than one. I convinced myself I couldn't show the entire me because I can be too much for some people.

Stop expecting people to indulge you when the entire time you should indulge yourself. You can't change your quirkiness, your laugh, the fact that you snore extremely loud, or how you make the room light up when you walk in. That is your light, and you deserve to live in that light. People who love you will accept that you talk a little too loud or you sometimes are a tad bit dramatic. Those are the people who matter. They won't say "I don't know why she/he is that way" they'll say "that's just who she/he is, and you got to love them."

Luckily, I have people who tell me when to stop apologizing. Somehow I still end up apologizing for apologizing too much. You are who the hell you are. As long as you're bettering yourself and growing in a way that's beneficial to your life, then that's all that matters. It's all about you and being true to who you are without question or doubt.

Too many times have I noticed I've sought outside validation to do certain things or speak on some issues because I have conditioned myself to believe maybe it's just me. That "if I say this they may not like me anymore." Guess what? Who the hell cares? If you do, you shouldn't because you are not here to dim your light to let others shine. Do you want to laugh? Laugh as loud as you can with no remorse.

Accepting who you are inside and whether or not people will accept or decline you is not your concern but, recognizing who you are and walking in your truth is. People often forget we don't need the validation of those around us to feel special. You being you is unique enough. There are so many things we have to settle for in life like bills, going to work, not being rich (you know the usual). You should not have to settle for a dimmer you especially at the demand of someone else.

Sometimes in the past where I silenced myself because I thought I was overreacting or would cause more harm because again "Tatyanna is too much." No, how you feel, what you have to say, how you react to bullshit is not too much. I've subjected myself to believe that I can't speak up or be who I am all for the sake of appealing to others.

I'm not apologizing for the fact that I'm the worst aux DJ in the world or how sometimes at the age of 25 I wish I could be a vampire because they're incredibly cool. I had an Invader Žim book bag with a hood my 12th-grade year in high school. I stopped wearing it because kids at school deemed me as childish/weird because of it. I have changed so much of myself to fit it in with people who didn't matter... even down to my sexuality.

What would you tell your younger self not to do? What advice would you give if you could give any, to the younger you about how you can be yourself? We have a world full of followers, zombies some people call them but, what makes you, you? What makes you different from the next person? What sets you aside as an individual? I believe most of us were born to stand out. Born to be the loudest ones in the room, the ones who laugh so obnoxiously it makes others laugh.

There are still times I've questioned myself so, no this is not perfect for me. I have times where I still think I am "too much." Not everyone will indulge, and some of us are a hard pill to swallow. Don't just be tolerated be loved by everyone in all aspects of you.

Nobody on this planet has the same set of fingerprints. So that should tell you being indeed who you are is unique. You want to scream at the top of your lungs? Feel free. You want to cry? Then cry as long as you can. Anything you do can never be too much for you. We all have our flaws, and yes some of them can be our characteristics but, it shouldn't be something we're ashamed of just something we should try to better.

No one can tell you how to do you better than you.

Be you. Do you.
And do so fucking unapologetically.

You Got Out Of Bed Today

The worst part about depression is how much it consumes you.

It feels like you can't breathe at the most inconvenient times

Like right now for instance. I'm at work sitting at my desk where everyone seems to love coming to because I always like a bit of "fun" to their long dragging days.

They all stop by this desk for a few laughs and another reason to smile that is my purpose that is what I do.

I have realized that even when an overwhelming feeling of sadness drapes over my head, I still feel the need to provide the entertainment.

Nobody ever realizes I'm fighting to every day to keep a smile on my face so they can keep a smile on theirs.

I am their hope, their happiness, but, I am not happy at all.

Every night when I go home, I like to finish a bottle of wine that I started when I come through the door.

Most of the time I drink cheap $2 bottles, my liver probably hates me.

I take 2 Benadryl's, finish my bottle that I did not use a glass for, and I wait until sleep conquers my depression.

I never recall what I dream about but, I'd like toast that it's something positive and pleasant.

I return to work the next day and make sure I put my smile on considering some people only have 9 hours to feel any bit of excitement.

When I walk into the office, they say "HEY GIRL WHAT DID YOU DO LAST NIGHT."

I tell them some wild story, throw in some jokes and watch their eyes get huge believing my lies.

I say "Girl whatever you do never mix dark and light alcohol," and I sit down exhausted.

They all laugh not knowing the drowsiness every morning spurs from the insomnia concoctions at night.

The worst part about wanting to pause your life is watching yourself spiral out of control emotionally and knowing you have to go through it all.

I want to be someone

I want to be something

I want to be enough

I want to be everything

I want to be great

I want to be great so bad that it sends me into a depression. You know those women you see, strong, black, gorgeous women.

They either just wrote a best seller or became entrepreneurs.

They always give the same speeches

They say life was tough but, they never took no for an answer.

They fought, and they won.

They don't tell you they also had luck on their side as well.

I want to be one of those women. I want it all. I want to be the best.

I'm just a funny girl who battles depression

I want to be more than that. I want to inspire, I have inspired, I want to speak about my battles.

I want people to know this is possible. I don't want to lie about my happiness. I want to BE happy.

- Sky Paints

One day I made a twitter thread about

how people should check on the people that check on them. You know the people who you go to vent and go to for advice? Believe it or not, everyone struggles with life from time to time, and it would be nice to have a listening ear. Most times people don't even want advice.

If you know like I know depression is not "cool," and people who suffer are suffering. Stop looking at people who battle depression as weak minded because they aren't. I can't say I suffer from depression but, I've dated someone who has and had my share of episodes like the next person.

Quick story. There was this person I dated who suffered from depression, and since I had never dealt with those issues, I did not know what I was doing. They were drinking a lot, they weren't sleeping, they weren't touching me anymore, and instead of being there I made it about our relationship. Instead of asking what is wrong with you I asked: "why don't you touch me anymore." I didn't at the time realize the impact I was making.

How could I though? I never experienced this type of relationship. It wasn't a manual on how to help people cope when they're stressed. I see there were other ways to help a little and, I say I could've done more or I could've listened more. The truth is I don't know what I could have done.

I had a friend who is currently dating someone who suffers from depression tell me she took up classes to help her loved one cope. Which, is a great idea. At some point, we all need someone whether we like to believe it. We all need friends, love, and people to hold us when we're drowning from the own sorrows we can't escape from.

It's hard trust me I know, I've always been this favorable light. I've always been happy but, these last few years I've battled more sadness than happiness. I tried to commit suicide twice so, I got a glimpse of what so many people face every day.

Depression comes in so many forms. It comes in drinking, laughter, sex, smoking, and sleeping. The people around you have more stories and secrets that they'd like you to believe.

If you battle depression, I want to remind you that you being here is important to me. Even if we've never spoken or I've never seen you a day in my life you are worth it. You're worth the fight. You're worth getting up every day even though moving out of bed can be one of the hardest things you've ever done. Those around you love you more than you realize. You're not a burden and the world will not be a better place without your presence.

Those who have lost loved ones to this battle. They didn't want to harm you. They didn't want you to hurt you, and it wasn't "selfish" of them to leave. It's not about you, it never was, and it never will be. Don't guilt yourself into thinking there was more you could've done because sometimes there isn't. Sometimes depression drowns them so much it's unbearable.

We all battle our own demons, and the hardest battles are the ones we can't speak about. The ones some of us don't know even where to begin to fix. Depression is not a choice and many people I encounter daily state these things. It's sickening because they won't understand until they've walked in your shoes. Don't expect them to understand and don't get upset when they don't. We sometimes only see things from our perspectives, and that's okay. You can't blame people for not being there when sometimes we don't realize what is happening to you or can't understand what is happening either.

I was lucky enough to have two beautiful young women who helped me through my depressive episode. The chat we were in was called "Safe Haven." We pulled each other through a lot. Whether it was daily text reminding us how great we were, random trips to check on one another, or the occasional 3-way conversation they pulled me through it, and I can guarantee you have people like that for you. It's okay to ask for help when you need help. We all need help, I've needed help, and I'm not ashamed to admit it.

Your story isn't over, and it isn't the end. You're book and chapter is more beautiful than you could ever imagine. Your life is a gift, and we all take it for granted sometimes. I can't tell you it'll be easy for anyone and that's to people who suffer and people who love those who suffer. It'll be roller coasters of difficulties, and sometimes we take more losses than wins. But, the triumphs, you hold on to those. You let those be the reason you want to wake up every day and put your pants on.

Trust me; I am not a person who can give you a fix for your problems because I have had my own share. But, let people be there for you whether you want the help or not. You're not alone, and you'll never be alone.

The sun doesn't always shine when you want.

Find light in the darkness of your tunnels.

It won't always last I promise.

You're enough for you.

Never forget it.

I love you.

You're Worthy Homie

Why do we think we don't deserve the love that has been given to us? Do we realize we're self-destructing your happiness? Do we not believe we cannot be loved because no one would be crazy enough to love us? You ever asked why someone likes you or what did you do to deserve a person who cares for you in ways that you've never been cared for? We are so hard on ourselves to the point where we feel it's impossible to have someone genuinely loves us due to our human flaws.

Honestly, are we that fucked up to think we don't deserve happiness? To think that for someone to love us that they have to be just as fucked up? Everyone talks about giving love and showing love to those around them but, no one ever talks about receiving it and receiving it without question. I can tell you every lousy characteristic of myself. I can tell you how I used to be a habitual liar or how I pushed everyone who wanted to help me away. I can tell you about how I still battle demons from nights that left me scarred forever. But, does that mean I cannot be loved?

How many times have you let someone open you up and show you things about yourself that you never knew? When you reflect, and you're haunted by all the wrong things you have done, does that somehow equate you'll never find happiness? Time after time again people have poured into me. Confessed their undying love and you know what I did about 99% of the time? I ran. I never felt I was worthy of love because I didn't allow it to be given.

We talk about reciprocation, and we talk about all the undying need to have people treat/love us the same way we love them but, sabotage it, and we do so mostly subconsciously. We get the woman or man of our dreams, and we do things like hurt them or lie to them or cheat on them. We pray to God for "forever love" but, when we get it, it is as if we can't handle it.

Sometimes we are own enemy, and we cause the downfall in a lot of the failed relationships in our life. You ever sat and thought yourself the most toxic person to you, is you? That maybe we can't receive love because you know deep down we don't love ourselves enough for somebody else to love us unconditionally. You don't think you deserve someone who loves you without conditions, expectations, or genuineness?

I mean yes, we are shocked when someone loves us to where it scares us. That type of love is the scariest because it is so raw and so untainted. It's pure, and you know that vulnerability is there. You've given someone the power to tear you apart. Shitless scary right? But, you deserve it. You deserve to wake up to a million text about how perfect you are, how much you mean to a person. You deserve roses at your job and surprise dates. You deserve someone to see your heart in the purest form of intimacy imaginable.

Stop finding reasons for you to be wrong for them. Often I hear people say this cliché excuse "I don't deserve you" or "You're better off without me." I get it; you feel like they are to genuine and too pure for you. Like they won't truly love you for your mood swings, family issues, or your overall human flaws. But, you can adapt to your environment if you wanted to.

Someone deciding to love you is not

your choice. You don't get to choose who gets to love you and who doesn't. You don't get to know the underlying why's. You don't get to decide when love should or should not be conditional. You don't get to choose anything other than loving them in return. Because a person who wants to love you will love you regardless of what you believe about yourself. You are your own worse critic, and sometimes we see ourselves in the worst light possible. It's impossible not to have questions, and why's. It's okay to ask for reassurance on why someone loves you only if you need to be reminded for yourself. Someone who loves you can and will answer everything you ask including the ones you don't ask.

People have this weird assumption that we can control who loves us or who we love and we can't. I could meet a stranger in the grocery store tomorrow and love them more than anyone I've ever dated. Life is too short not to want to be loved. You cannot survive without it. Unlike many of my peers who believe the opposite love is the only universal language that we all understand.

I want you to smile because you've allowed someone to love you truly. You've allowed someone to see you with your wig braids or lousy haircut days. You've allowed someone to surprise you with lunch or order your food the exact way you would regardless of how complicated it is. I want you to smile because you've been so vulnerable that it feels like you've shed your skin for the first time. I want you to be happy because you know what it means to be understood. They know to give you space when you're irritable. They know when you get upset you're anti, but they come and sit in silence with you.

Love the person who can pick out your meals while you're in the bathroom, the person who won't forget to grab 1% milk because you're a little lactose. The person who knows to get everything on the side for you chipotle because it's kind of nasty when you reheat it with the sour cream. The person who will remember to tell you to set your alarm 30 minutes earlier because you're not a morning person. Love that person who knows what you will say before you even open your mouth and let that person love you.

Stop fighting everything because at one point everything you knew about love came crashing down or because your mom/dad didn't love you properly growing up. That is not your ending to love because it's all around you. You deserve the happiness or happy ending you haven't gotten anywhere else. Again, true love will scare you shitless. That amount of vulnerability on both ends can destroy you if given to the wrong person. Trust me, I understand. But, the beauty of it is when it's true, you won't be destroyed.

I won't sit here and pretend this will be all rainbows and unicorns. There will be tough days where you don't know anymore. Sometimes, love like that doesn't work out, and it is okay because all your life you've been searching for an example of love, a right example. The silver lining is that you felt it and experienced it so, now the bar has risen, and you know you're worthy. You're worthy of the work it is to have someone love you.

So now, you no longer be in love, you become it, and with that, you become more open, more vulnerable, and your discernment becomes clearer.

You are now the love you once didn't think you deserved.

Who's Doing The Work Though?

I hear so many people who say they want to do better or be better people, but when the universe gives them a test, the easily revert backward. The change will not come overnight and nor will you ever stop changing. The world is moving so rapidly, things are continually evolving, and you are evolving. How in breath do most people say they want to improve their circumstance but, won't do the work?

The definition of insanity is doing the

same thing over and over and expecting a different outcome. You want a better job but, you don't want to fill out job applications. You want to be more emotionally balanced but, you don't meditate or calm yourself down before reacting. Impulse is normal we want to go with the animal instinct. We want to go off when someone hurts our feelings. It's normal to feel that way but, how far has that gotten you?

In this book, we talk about growth, growth for your spirit and growth for your mind. But, for some reason, we do nothing to grow. We spend little time to ourselves, we don't listen to our thoughts throughout the day, and we don't even take mental breaks when we're overwhelmed. We don't learn our boundaries, and some still aren't as honest with ourselves as we should be.

I'm not saying it's easy by far because it is not but, you have to put in the manpower to get the results. You want to learn yourself inside and out? Start with being honest, not only to you but those around you. Most of the time, your loved ones will either agree or tell you that you're in denial. Listen to them because they are eight times out of 10 pointing out things you can't see for yourself.

Will you need help? Yes. That's what books and other people who you can learn from are for. Whether it's a therapist, a mentor, or your wise ass best friend you can find someone to keep you on track. Will it be hard? Yes. Will you have days where you feel stagnant? Yes. But, is it worth it? Yes. I'm still learning as I go. I will never stop learning. I had to make serious life changes though.

I had to pray more, and I had to cry more, I had to write a freaking book about it. There was a time where I was complacent in who I was. You know, the whole "that's how I am and accept me" concept. Which was the shittier version of me I may add? I eventually looked in the mirror and finally said: "get your shit together, Tot." Do I have days where I sometimes mess up? Heck yeah. Do I learn and say "girl you were dramatic"? Yes. Growing takes sacrifice. You may even cut a few friends off along the way because you're operating differently.

Things that once excited you no longer excites you and conversations become less entertaining because to you they lack substance. Some people won't understand this, and it's okay. It's all about putting in the work to secure that you will become a better you. You'll have people who'll tear you down and remind you of every bad thing you ever did. You'll have people doubt you and say you can't change which is okay because people who aren't growing can't accept that you are.

Kill them with love. Don't allow them to get under your skin, pray for them, and continue to love them even if it has to be from a distance. Growth is a hell of a lot of work and it'll be days where you want just let it all fall back. You'll be tested but, you must always be the bigger person, and you'll even have occasional emotional breaks. We all have them.

I can't say I came to this point on my own. I did a lot of the work myself but, I have a great group of friends and a loving family. Most of them held me together in ways I couldn't do so myself. But, I continued to do the work.

I began listening to podcasts and reading more books. I started to meditate, and I attempted this morning routine, but it ended horribly. Hey look everything doesn't always work but, you should always attempt. If you want to do yoga, do yoga, loc your hair, write a book, or hit the gym. Do anything that gives you calmness. Anything that lets the outside voices or the negative thoughts be pushed aside, do it. Do you want peace? You want quietness? Well you will have to fight every day for it until it becomes who you are. Until the silence is no longer scary and outsiders have no affects your mood.

Remember if you're comfortable you're not doing enough. Growth makes you uncomfortable and makes you want to get up and fix your entire life. It'll never be a point of complacency for you, ever. Don't expect that. Once you open the door, closing it is no longer an option.

Guard your heart, learn your boundaries,

and if you can, help others along the way. Be the change you want to see in the world and other people. You will run into roadblocks but, figure how to work through them rather than around them. As I said, it will never be easy for you. It was difficult for me. I had to start from scratch but, it was worth it. All I see in my life is love and happiness. Is everything perfect? No, and it will never be perfect but, it's my version of beauty. It's my imperfect ideal story.

I am who I am, and I'm still who I was. I just learned to operate within the better version of myself.

The End

I can't say that everything I learned was intentional. Most of the gems I came across were entirely trial and error or speaking to a random person in the street. Who I became wasn't a mistake I was meant to meet the people who broke and healed me. Karma also had a bit to do with it too. (she's such a ruthless little bitch.)

But, she was the bitch I need to evolve into what I am today, and that is love. In all aspects I am love. I am the love I never got, the love I forgot to give, and the love to make me see. I started by being the soul with no purpose and no real destination to where I was going. I hated love for what she brought me. But, love is abstract it's been what it has always been we just have negative experiences.

To say that it's not the reason some of us are here today would be preposterous. To say that love is not a universal language in whatever place you're in would be a lie. I've learned to operate in every version of myself because I'm not just one thing. I am a mom, a woman, a friend, a daughter, a sister, a companion, a lover, a healer, a writer, and the list goes on. To operate in one portion of me is an injustice of who I worked so hard to become.

There were days I sat and asked myself how do I become the love that I searched so hard to find? How do I get to the point of no matter what version of someone else's love is given to me; I don't allow it to change who I am?

The answer is reflection.

I reflected on all the damage I've caused and looked at the energy that I put into the world. From my sisters that have been there since I was 16 years old to relationships with my mother. Then, I thought about the pain that was brought to me and realized that I wasn't the victim. I was but, not really if that makes sense. I spent a year of my life crying trying to figure out how something that felt so right became so wrong? In a previous chapter, I talked about apologies. I failed to mention that the pain that was brought to me I caused to someone else.

Some of you know how it feels to change everything negative about yourself for love and then that same love destroying you beyond measures. It's the breakdown to be rebuild. It is pain before the beauty. The woman now loves the woman I used to be because without her I am nothing. Without her, the lessons, the tears, and the laughs I wouldn't be possible.

She was mine. The girl who lied habitually and talked to people she loved as if they were nothing, treated people as if they were disposable. The using, the emotional manipulation, the codependency, the hate, the anger, the desire for sex and using people as nothing more than orgasms. She was fucking mine.

Every lesson since the age of 15 has prepared me to be who I am today which is a strong, bold, independent, caring woman. To be a woman of such depth is a shocker because I was heading down a dark path. People who have watched me grow often tell me it's beautiful, and to them it is but, to me it was inevitable.

The first thing to save me was becoming a mom and the second thing to evolve me was a heartbreak. I can't tell you how or why life happened that way it did for me but, it did, and I am eternally grateful. I have been torn apart and also tore apart. I've cried and caused tears. I've fought and been fought. I've taken and also have given. No one on this earth is perfect, and perfection isn't beauty. Flaws are.

Be so transparent that you allow anyone who comes in contact with you feel vulnerable as well. Become the confidant that you need in times of confusion. Which sounds weird because you would assume someone outside of yourself but, no you are the confidant. I have friends who are also my confidants but; I consult myself first and last. Talk to yourself always because you will never steer yourself wrong.

Watch how you talk to yourself though. Start by manifesting what you want even if you have no real faith start by believing in you. It's incredible to me to see when I focused on healing myself I became on own conduit.

To all my healers some of us believe that we are meant to heal ourselves. Who heals the healer? The answer is everyone who you've healed. Conversations we have with people looking for guidance aren't just for them it's for us. The people who have called me a light don't realize they are also my light. Feeding them with what the need feeds me simultaneously.

The person who heals the healer isn't one but, all.

Every person I've come in contact with has taught me a lesson to bring me where I am now.

I am love, and I am so filled by it because I allowed myself to become it. Not for myself alone but, for those who are trying to find it. I make friends to give them an example of what friendship should feel like even if my time in their life is limited. I meet lovers who fall for me not because I'm attractive, smart, or funny but because I'm raw and I'm open. I want each person who encounters me to experience me because I am an experience and I know that. I know I'm not a lifetime commitment to every person I encounter and I've accepted it.

She was mine to grow but, to also share.

I can leave this earth knowing that some portion of who I became has impacted the people I've allowed into my realm. Knowing it has in some way started their journey to be the better version of themselves comforts me in ways I can't express.

Become the butterfly in the wind.

Become the flower that blooms when it's needed.

Keep your heart pure because nothing can tarnish what's real gold.

Lastly, share the love that you found in you with others who need it.

She was mine, mine to bare, mine to heal, and mine to grow.

You are yours.

What's greater? Your urge to grow or your resistance to change?

Let that resonate.

Acknowledgments:

Safe Have, Sky Paints, Eb, & 5'Oclock

To the countless souls I have engaged with… I don't think I could have finished this without you all.
Even down to just letting me read to you.

Much appreciation and much gratitude

I Love You

CPSIA information can be obtained
at www.ICGtesting.com
Printed in the USA
BVHW071246280119
538842BV00004B/466/P